Book Repo
Forms

Bears
Book Report Form

Literature Skill Focus: Determining if a story is real or make-believe

1. Reading at School

- Read *Klondike & Snow* to your class. This is the story of two abandoned polar bear cubs that were raised by the staff of the Denver Zoo. Ask students if the things in the book might actually happen. Lead them to the conclusion that the photographs and content of this book indicate it is a true story.

- Read *Brown Bear, Brown Bear, What Do You See?* This is a classic rhyming picture book. On each page, readers meet a new animal who introduces the animal on the next page. Ask students if this story is real. Have them give specific examples from the story that support their opinions. Lead them to see that this book is make-believe.

2. Reading at Home

- Have students choose a book about bears from the library. They take the book home to share with their parents. Together, the parents and child complete the form on page 3, and the child returns it to school.

3. Sharing the Book Reports

- Have students sit in a circle holding their completed book report forms. Briefly review the differences between real and make-believe books. Place the two books you read to the class in the center of the circle.

- Invite students to share the name of the book they chose and tell whether it was a real or make-believe story. Have them stack their book report forms on top of the appropriate book. When all students have shared their books, count to see how many real and how many make-believe books were read. Record the results.

Good Books to Read

Make-Believe

Beardream by Will Hobbs

The Berenstain Bears and the Truth and other Berenstain Bears books by Stan and Jan Berenstain

Blueberries for Sal by Robert McCloskey

Brown Bear, Brown Bear, What Do You See? or *Panda Bear, Panda Bear, What Do You See?* by Bill Martin, Jr.

Jamberry by Bruce Degen

Little Bear and other Little Bear books by Elsa Holmelund Minarik

Time to Sleep by Denise Fleming

Real

Bears Are Curious by Joyce Milton

Bear Snores On by Karma Wilson

Klondike & Snow by David E. Kenny, Cynthia Bickel, and Dennis A. Roling

Where Do Bears Sleep? by Barbara Shook Hazen

How to Report on Books • EMC 6007 • © Evan-Moor Corp.

Name _____

Bears
Book Report Form

We read a good book about bears.

Title: _____

Author: _____

Illustrator: _____

The story was: real   make-believe

How could you tell? _____

_____

Dear Parents,
Read this book with your child. Talk about whether this book is a real or a make-believe story. Encourage your child to tell why the book is real or make-believe. Fill in the report form.

This book report is due back in class: _____   Parent Signature _____

Machines

Book Report Form

Literature Skill Focus: Determining if a story is real or make-believe

1. Reading at School

- Read *Tractor*. This book is full of big color photos of tractors, farm equipment, and farms. Ask students if the machines in the book are actual machines. Lead them to the conclusion that the information in the book is real.

- Read *Me and My Flying Machine*. This is the tale of a young boy who decides to build a plane in his barn. He imagines all the wonderful things he will accomplish in it. When his hopes are dashed, the boy is undaunted, and he immediately looks to the next challenge. Ask students if the machines in this book are actual machines. Have students give specific examples from the story to support their opinions. Lead them to the conclusion that this story is make-believe.

2. Reading at Home

- Have students choose a book about machines from the library. They take the book home to share with their parents. Together, the parents and child complete the form on page 5. The child returns it to school.

3. Sharing the Book Reports

- Have students sit in a circle holding their completed book report forms. Briefly review the differences between real and make-believe. Place the two books you read in the center of the circle.

- Invite students to share the name of the book they chose and tell whether the story was real or make-believe. Have them place their book report forms beside the appropriate model book. Then create a graph showing the make-believe books read and the real books read.

Good Books to Read

Make-Believe

Can You See What I See? Dream Machine by Walter Wick

Humphrey, Albert, and the Flying Machine by Kathryn Lasky

Me and My Flying Machine by Marianna Mayer

Wilbur's Space Machine by Lorna Balian

Real

Building Machines and What They Do by Derek Radford

Dazzling Diggers by Tony Mitton

Kids' Book of Giant Machines by Erik A. Bruun and Karl Wiens

Machines at Work by Byron Barton

Tractor by Caroline Bingham

Name _____

Machines
Book Report Form

Title: _____

Author: _____

Illustrator: _____

The story was: real   make-believe

How could you tell? _____

_____

Dear Parents,
Read this book with your child. Talk about whether this book is real or make-believe. Encourage your child to tell why the book is real or make-believe. Fill in the report form.

This book report is due back in class: _____   Parent Signature _____

Cats

Book Report Form

Literature Skill Focus: Naming the characters in a story

1. Reading at School

- Explain to students that the people and animals in books are called the characters. Read *Angus and the Cat.* This book features Angus the Scottie dog, who tries to outwit the family cat. The underlying theme is how easy it is to get lost. Have students identify the book's characters. List the characters on a chart or board with a simple drawing beside each one.

2. Reading at Home

- Students choose a book about cats from the library. They take the book home to share with their parents. Together, the parents and child complete the form on page 7. The child returns it to school.

3. Sharing the Book Reports

- Have students sit in a circle holding their completed book report forms. Ask students to recall what the term *character* means.

- Invite students to share the name of the book they chose and name the characters in the story. When all students have shared, point out that every story had the same character—a cat!

Good Books to Read

Angus and the Cat by Marjorie Flack

Barn Cat by Carol P. Saul

Cat & Mouse: A Delicious Tale by Jiwon Oh

The Cat Who Walked Across France by Kate Banks

Cross-Country Cat by Mary Calhoun

The Fire Cat by Esther Averill

Five Creatures by Emily Jenkins

The Grannyman by Judith Byron Schachner

Have You Seen My Cat? by Eric Carle

I Am the Dog I Am the Cat by Donald Hall

I Walk at Night by Lois Duncan

Millions of Cats by Wanda Gag

Mr. Putter & Tabby Pour the Tea by Cynthia Rylant

Nicky the Jazz Cat by Carol Friedman

Three Samurai Cats: A Story from Japan by Eric A. Kimmel

When Cats Dream by Dav Pilkey

Name _____

Cats
Book Report Form

We read a good book about cats.

Title: _____

Author: _____

Illustrator: _____

The characters in this book are: _____

_____

Which character would you like to meet?

_____

Dear Parents,
Read this book with your child. Talk about the characters in the book. List them on the form. Discuss which character your child would like to meet. Fill in the report form.

This book report is due back in class: _____   Parent Signature _____

Dogs
Book Report Form

Literature Skill Focus: Identifying the main character in a story

1. Reading at School
- Briefly review the term *character*. Explain that usually a book has one or two important, or main, characters.

- Read the book *Harry the Dirty Dog*. This is the story of a white dog with black spots. He hates getting a bath, so he buries the scrubbing brush in the backyard. He gets so dirty that he becomes a black dog with white spots.

- Ask students to identify the main character in the book. Have them explain why the character they named is important.

2. Reading at Home
- Have students choose a book about dogs from the library. They take the book home to read with their parents. The parents and child complete the form on page 9. The child returns it to school.

3. Sharing the Book Reports
- Have students sit in a circle holding their completed book report forms. Remind students that the main character is the most important character in the story.

- Invite students to share the name of the book they read, name the main character, and tell something that the main character did.

Good Books to Read

The Adventures of Taxi Dog by Debra and Sal Barracca

Buster by Denise Fleming

Dog Heaven by Cynthia Rylant

Go, Dog. Go! by P. D. Eastman

Good Dog, Carl and other Carl books by Alexandra Day

Harry the Dirty Dog by Gene Zion

Henry and Mudge: The First Book of Their Adventures by Cynthia Rylant

Hondo & Fabian by Peter McCarty

Martha Speaks and other Martha books by Susan Meddaugh

Measuring Penny by Loreen Leedy

Meet the Barkers: Morgan and Moffat Go to School by Tomie dePaola

Meow! by Katya Arnold

Officer Buckle and Gloria by Peggy Rathmann

The Poky Little Puppy by Janette Sebring Lowrey

The Stray Dog by Marc Simont

How to Report on Books • EMC 6007 • © Evan-Moor Corp.

Name _____

Dogs
Book Report Form

Title: _____

Author: _____

Main character in the book: _____

Why is this character the most important character?

_____

_____

Dear Parents,
Read this book with your child. Have your child identify the main character. Talk about what the character looked like and what the character did in the story. Decide why that character is the main character. Fill in the report form.

This book report is due back in class: _____   Parent Signature _____

Hats
Book Report Form

Literature Skill Focus: Describing the main character

1. Reading at School

- Point out to students that there is often one character in a story that is the most important. Explain that this character is called the main character.

- Read *Milo's Hat Trick*. This is the story of Milo the magician, who can't do any tricks at all. He can't even pull a rabbit out of a hat. He finds a bear to pull out of a hat, but the bear gets tired from popping in and out of the hat 762 times.

- Ask students to identify the main character in the book. Have students tell why they think Milo is the main character. Then ask students to describe Milo. Help them develop a list of adjectives and phrases that describe him.

2. Reading at Home

- Have students choose a book about hats from the library. They take the book home to share with their parents. Together, the parents and child complete the form on page 11. The child returns it to school.

3. Sharing the Book Reports

- Have students sit in a circle holding their completed book report forms. Remind students that the main character is the most important one in the story.

- Invite students to share the name of the book they chose, name the main character, and describe the character.

- When all students have reported on their books, point out that the main characters' names are sometimes part of the book title.

Good Books to Read

The 500 Hats of Bartholomew Cubbins by Dr. Seuss

Caps for Sale by Esphyr Slobodkina

The Cat in the Hat by Dr. Seuss

Do You Have a Hat? by Eileen Spinelli

The Hat by Jan Brett

Milo's Hat Trick by Jon Agee

Shall I Knit You a Hat?: A Christmas Yarn by Kate Klise

How to Report on Books • EMC 6007 • © Evan-Moor Corp.

Name _____

Hats
Book Report Form

Title: _____

Author: _____

Main character's name: _____

Circle words that tell about the character.

kind	loud	shy	brave
sad	happy	friendly	sick
mean	busy	afraid	hardworking
playful	funny	smart	lazy

Dear Parents,
Read this book with your child. Talk about the main character in the story. Help your child describe the character by circling words on the form. Fill in the report form.

This book report is due back in class: _____ Parent Signature _____

Houses
Book Report Form

Literature Skill Focus: Identifying where a story takes place

1. Reading at School

• Read *Mr. Pine's Purple House*. This story is about Mr. Pine, who lives in a white house in a neighborhood of white houses. He wants to make his house stand out, so he paints it purple. All of his neighbors end up painting their houses a different color.

• Ask students where the story takes place. If appropriate, tell students that the setting is where and when the story takes place. This lesson focuses on the "where" part of the setting.

2. Reading at Home

• Have students choose a book about houses from the library. They take the book home to share with their parents. The parents and child complete the form on page 13. The child returns it to school.

3. Sharing the Book Reports

• Make signs that have several different settings, such as "In a house," "By a lake," "On a farm," etc.

• Have students sit in a circle holding their completed book report forms.

• Invite students to share the name of the book they chose and tell where the story happened. Have them place their completed book report next to the sign that tells where the story happened.

• When all students have reported on their books, look at the signs and book reports. Lead students to the conclusion that all of the stories took place in a house.

Good Books to Read

A House Is a House for Me by Mary Ann Hoberman

The House That Jack Built by Simms Taback

The Little House by Virginia Lee Burton

Mouse in the House and others by Henrietta

Mr. Pine's Purple House by Leonard Kessler

The Napping House by Audrey and Don Wood

Sunflower House by Eve Bunting

How to Report on Books • EMC 6007 • © Evan-Moor Corp.

Name _____

Houses
Book Report Form

Title: _____

Author: _____

Illustrator: _____

Where did the story take place? _____

Could the story happen at your house? _____

_____

Dear Parents,
Read this book with your child. Talk about where the story happened. Think about whether the story could happen at your house. Fill in the report form.

This book report is due back in class: _____   Parent Signature _____

Weather
Book Report Form

Literature Skill Focus: Recalling details in a story

1. Reading at School

- Read *Katy and the Big Snow*. Katy is a red crawler tractor. When a blizzard dumps snow on her town, Katy turns into a snowplow and saves the day.

- Ask students to tell what the weather is like in the story. Lead them to the conclusion that the weather is important to the story.

2. Reading at Home

- Have students choose a book about weather from the library. They take the book home to share with their parents. Together, the parents and child complete the form on page 15. The child returns it to school.

3. Sharing the Book Reports

- Have students sit in a circle holding their completed book report forms. Brainstorm different kinds of weather. Record the students' ideas on a chart with picture symbols and words.

- Invite students to share the name of the book they chose and tell what kind of weather was in the book. Make a tally mark beside the appropriate weather symbol and word on the chart as students share their books.

Good Books to Read

Brewster the Rain-Makin' Rooster by Tim Ross

Bringing the Rain to Kapiti Plain by Verna Aardema

Cloudy With a Chance of Meatballs by Judi Barrett

First Snow by Emily Arnold McCully

Katy and the Big Snow by Virginia Lee Burton

Kipper's Sunny Day by Mick Inkpen

Oh Say Can You Say What's the Weather Today? by Tish Rabe

Rain Makes Applesauce by Julian Scheer

Sun Bread by Elisa Kleven

How to Report on Books • EMC 6007 • © Evan-Moor Corp.

Name _____

Weather
Book Report Form

Title: _____

Author: _____

Illustrator: _____

What is the weather like in the story?_____

Would you like to be in the story? _____

_____

Dear Parents,
Read this book with your child. Talk about the weather in the story. Ask your child whether he or she would like to be in the story. Encourage your child to tell why or why not. Fill in the report form.

This book report is due back in class: _____   Parent Signature _____

Grasshoppers
Book Report Form

Literature Skill Focus: Retelling a story in sequence

1. Reading at School
- Write the words *first, next,* and *last* on a chart. Ask students to listen to find out what happens first, next, and last in the story you read.

- Read *The Ant and the Grasshopper.* This is an Aesop's fable reset in China. The ants are preparing for winter while the grasshopper sings and dances. Have students retell the story by telling what happened first, next, and last.

2. Reading at Home
- Have students choose a book about grasshoppers from the library. They take the book home to share with their parents. Together, the parents and child complete the form on page 17. The child returns it to school.

3. Sharing the Book Reports
- Have students sit in a circle holding their completed book report forms. Review the idea of retelling a story by reporting what happened first, next, and last.

- Invite students to share the name of their book and to retell the story.

Good Books to Read

The Ant and the Grasshopper by Amy Lowry Poole

Are You a Grasshopper? by Judy Allen

Grasshopper Pie by Rebecca Talley

Imani's Music by Sheron Williams

Leaving Home with a Pickle Jar by Barbara Dugan

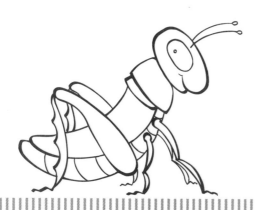

How to Report on Books • EMC 6007 • © Evan-Moor Corp.

Name _____

Grasshoppers
Book Report Form

Title: _____

Author: _____

What happened first? _____

_____

What happened next? _____

_____

What happened last? _____

_____

Dear Parents,
Read this book with your child. Talk about the events in the story. Have your child retell the story by telling what happened first, next, and last. Fill in the report form.

This book report is due back in class: _____   Parent Signature _____

Trucks
Book Report Form

Literature Skill Focus: Determining if part of a story is real or make-believe

1. Reading at School
- Read *Farmer Dale's Red Pickup Truck*. This rhyming story is about Farmer Dale, his old truck, and all the animals he picks up on the way to a talent show. By the time he arrives, the truck bulges with squabbling animals.

- Ask students to identify all the animals that were in the truck. Record their responses on a chart. Ask if each of those animals could really fit in a truck.

2. Reading at Home
- Have students choose a fiction book about trucks from the library. They take the book home to share with their parents. Together, the parents and child complete the form on page 19. The child returns it to school.

3. Sharing the Book Reports
- Have students sit in a circle holding their completed book report forms.

- Invite students to share the name of the book they chose and what the truck carried. Ask if that could really fit in a truck. Record their responses.

Good Books to Read

Curious George and the Dumptruck by H. A. Rey

Farmer Dale's Red Pickup Truck by Lisa Wheeler

My Truck Is Stuck! by Kevin Lewis

Stringbean's Trip to the Shining Sea by Vera B. Williams and Jennifer Williams

How to Report on Books • EMC 6007 • © Evan-Moor Corp.

Name _____

Trucks
Book Report Form

Title: _____

Author: _____

What did the truck carry in this book? _____

_____

Could that really fit in the truck? _____

_____

Dear Parents,
Read this book with your child. Talk about what the truck carried. Explore if that could really fit in a truck. Fill in the report form.

This book report is due back in class: _____   Parent Signature _____

How to Report on Books • EMC 6007 • © Evan-Moor Corp.

Robots
Book Report Form

Literature Skill Focus: Retelling a story

1. Reading at School

- Remind students that when they retell a story they need to tell about what happened in the beginning, in the middle, and at the end of the story.

- Read *The Berenstain Bear Scouts and the Run-Amuck Robot*. This is the story of Robow the robot of all work. The Scouts try to stop him before he sends all the residents of bear country running for cover. Ask students to retell each part of the story. Remind them to retell the beginning, the middle, and the end.

2. Reading at Home

- Have students choose a book about robots from the library. They take the book home to share with their parents. Together, the parents and child complete the form on page 21. The child returns it to school.

3. Sharing the Book Reports

- Have students sit in a circle holding their completed book report forms.

- Invite a few students to share the name of their book and to retell the story. Remind them to identify the beginning, middle, and end.

Good Books to Read

The Berenstain Bear Scouts and the Run-Amuck Robot by Stan, Jan, and Michael Berenstain

Cosmo and the Robot by Brian Pinkney

Hello, Robots by Bob Staake

Little Robot Rabbit by Michael Brownlow

Me and My Robot by Tracey West

Robots Slither by Ryan Ann Hunter

Name _____

Robots
Book Report Form

Title: _____

Author: _____

In the beginning of the book... _____

_____

In the middle of the book... _____

_____

At the end of the book... _____

_____

Dear Parents,
Read this book with your child. Talk about what happened in the story. Have your child retell the story by telling what happens
in the beginning, in the middle, and at the end. Fill in the report form.

This book report is due back in class: _____   Parent Signature _____

Ladybugs
Book Report Form

Literature Skill Focus: Retelling a story ending

1. Reading at School

- Ask students to tell you what an ending is. Read *The Very Lazy Ladybug*. This is the story of a ladybug who is so lazy that she doesn't even know how to fly. She wants to look for a new sleeping spot. She hitches rides from different passing animals.

- Have students draw a picture that shows the ending of the story. Then ask several students to tell about their drawings.

- Restate the ending of the story in words. Ask students whether they liked the ending or not. Have them support their choice by telling why.

2. Reading at Home

- Have students choose a book about ladybugs from the library. They take the book home to share with their parents. The parents and child complete the form on page 23. The child returns it to school.

3. Sharing the Book Reports

- Have students sit in a circle holding their completed book report forms. Invite a few students to share the name of their book and to retell the story's ending. Ask students to tell whether they liked the ending and why.

Good Books to Read

Five Little Ladybugs by Karyn Henley

The Grouchy Ladybug by Eric Carle

Ladybug, Ladybug by Ruth Brown

Ladybug on the Move by Richard Fowler

Ladybug's Birthday by Steve Metzger

Little Buggy by Kevin O'Malley

The Very Lazy Ladybug by Isobel Finn and Jack Tickle

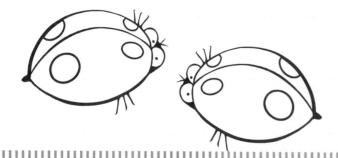

How to Report on Books • EMC 6007 • © Evan-Moor Corp.

Name _____

Ladybugs
Book Report Form

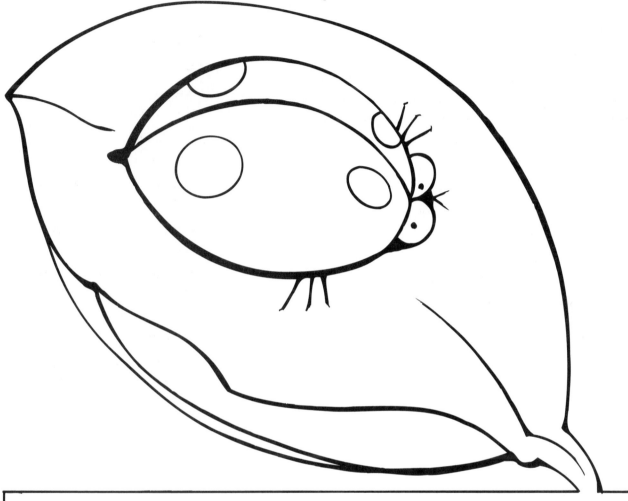

Title: _____

Author: _____

Did you like the ending of this story?   yes   no

Tell why or why not. _____

_____

_____

Dear Parents,
Read this book with your child. Talk about the ending of the story. Have your child draw a picture on the form to show the ending. Discuss whether he or she liked the ending. Encourage your child to tell why or why not. Fill in the report form.

This book report is due back in class: _____   Parent Signature _____

Tails
Book Report Form
Literature Skill Focus: Making up an alternate ending

1. Reading at School
- Read *How the Manx Cat Lost Its Tail*. This tale is based on the story of Noah's ark. As the animals board the ark, Noah notices that the Manx cat is missing. His wife shows him and his sons how to call a cat. The kitty slips onboard just as the door is closing, and its tail is snipped off.

- Have students retell the ending to the story. Then ask students to think of other endings that Janet Stevens might have used in her book.

2. Reading at Home
- Have students choose a book about tails from the library. They take the book home to share with their parents. Together, the parents and child complete the form on page 25. The child returns it to school.

3. Sharing the Book Reports
- Have students sit in a circle holding their completed book report forms.

- Invite students to share the name of the book they chose and tell how the story ended. Then have them suggest one new ending for the story.

- You may need to allow several share-and-tell sessions for this activity.

Good Books to Read

How the Manx Cat Lost Its Tail by Janet Stevens

Mouse Tail Moon by Joanne Ryder

The Perfect Tail: A Fred and Lulu Story by Mie Araki

A Pika's Tail by Sally Plumb

The Rabbit's Tail: A Story from Korea by Suzanne Crowder Han

The Spooky Tail of Prewitt Peacock by Bill Peet

Tale of a Tail by Judit Z. Bodnar

Why Epossumondas Has No Hair on His Tail by Coleen Salley

Name _____

Tails
Book Report Form

Title: _____

Author: _____

The book ended when... _____

_____

Another way the story could end is... _____

_____

Dear Parents,
Read this book with your child. Talk about the ending of the story. Together, think of several alternate endings. Fill in the report form.

This book report is due back in class: _____   Parent Signature _____

Big Machines
Book Report Form

Literature Skill Focus: Recalling information from a story

1. Reading at School

• Ask students to listen closely as you read *Tractor* or another nonfiction book about big machines.

• Have students recall something they have learned by listening to the book. List their contributions on a chart. Explain that the statements are called facts because they are true.

2. Reading at Home

• Have students choose a nonfiction book about big machines from the library. They take the book home to share with their parents. Together, the parents and child complete the form on page 27. The child returns it to school.

3. Sharing the Book Reports

• Have students sit in a circle holding their completed book report forms. Briefly review with students that a fact is a true statement about a topic.

• Invite students to share the name of the book they chose and tell one fact they learned when they read the book.

• List all of the facts on a chart. Have students draw appropriate illustrations next to each fact.

Good Books to Read

The Adventures of Bob and Red by David Barron

All Aboard! A True Train Story by Susan Kuklin

Arthur's Tractor: A Fairy Tale with Mechanical Parts by Pippa Goodhart

Jingle the Brass by Patricia Newman

The Little Engine That Could by Watty Piper

Night Train by Caroline Stutson

The Rusty, Trusty Tractor by Joy Cowley

Seymour Simon's Book of Trains by Seymour Simon

Shortcut by Donald Crews

Tractor by Caroline Bingham

Tractor by Craig McFarland Brown

Trains by Gail Gibbons

Tremendous Tractors by Tony Mitton

Two Little Trains by Margaret Wise Brown

Name _____

Big Machines
Book Report Form

Title: _____

Author: _____

I learned these three things from the book:

1. _____

2. _____

3. _____

Dear Parents,
Read this book with your child. Talk about the information included in the story. Help your child think of three things he or she learned by reading the book. Fill in the report form.

This book report is due back in class: _____ Parent Signature _____

Balloons
Book Report Form

Literature Skill Focus: Recalling information from a story

1. Reading at School

- Read *A Rainbow Balloon: A Book of Concepts*. This book contains beautiful color photos of hot-air balloons, as well as fundamental information on how they fly.

- Ask students to tell something they learned as they were listening to the book. Record the information in large balloons drawn on a chart.

2. Reading at Home

- Have students choose a book about balloons from the library. They take the book home to share with their parents. Together, the parents and child complete the form on page 29. The student returns it to school.

3. Sharing the Book Reports

- Have students sit in a circle holding their completed book report forms. Invite students to share the name of the book they chose and to tell something they learned by reading the book.

- Record the information on a chart.

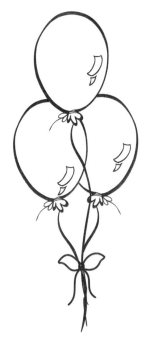

Good Books to Read

The Amazing Air Balloon by Jean Van Leeuwen and Marco Ventura

Beaten by a Balloon by Margaret Mahy

The Blue Balloon by Mick Inkpen

Cinderella and the Hot Air Balloon by Ann Jungman and Russell Ayto

Curious George and the Hot Air Balloon by H. A. Rey

A Rainbow Balloon: A Book of Concepts by Ann Lenssen

The Red Balloon by Albert Lamorisse

You Can't Take a Balloon into the Museum of Fine Arts and *You Can't Take a Balloon into the National Gallery* by Jacqueline Preiss Weitzman

How to Report on Books • EMC 6007 • © Evan-Moor Corp.

Name _____

Balloons
Book Report Form

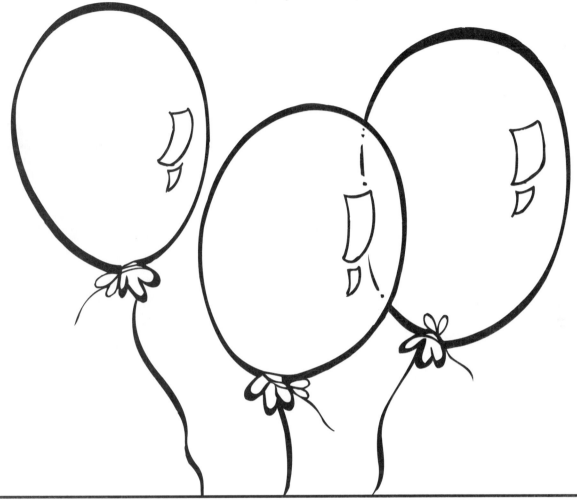

Title: _____

Author: _____

I learned these facts: _____

_____

_____

_____

Dear Parents,
Read this book with your child. Talk about the information in the book. Help your child think of three facts he or she learned by reading the book. Fill in the report form.

This book report is due back in class: _____   Parent Signature _____

Authors
Book Report Form

Literature Skill Focus: Learning about an author

1. Reading at School
- Choose several books from your library that include author biographies.
- Show students where the information about the authors' lives is found. Read the information and discuss it.

2. Reading at Home
- Have students choose a book with an author biography from the library. They take the book home to share with their parents. Together, the parents and child complete the form on page 31. The child returns it to school.

3. Sharing the Book Reports
- Have students sit in a circle holding their completed book report forms. Have a chart ready to record information about each author.
- Invite students to share the name of the book they chose and tell one thing about the book's author. Record the authors' names and information on the chart.

Good Books to Read

Blueberries for Sal by Robert McCloskey

Corduroy by Don Freeman

Mike Mulligan and His Steam Shovel by Virginia Lee Burton

Millions of Cats by Wanda Gag

Mommies Say Shhh! by Patricia Polacco

The Snowy Day by Ezra Jack Keats

Where the Wild Things Are by Maurice Sendak

Name _____

Authors
Book Report Form

The person who writes a book is called an author.

Title: _____

Author's first name: _____

Author's last name: _____

Is the author a man or a woman? _____

Write one thing you learned about the author. _____

_____

_____

Making Pictures
Book Report Form

Literature Skill Focus: Learning about an author/illustrator

1. Reading at School

- Choose several books from your library that were written and illustrated by the same person. Show students a few pictures in each book. Tell them that a person who creates pictures for books is called an illustrator. Show students where the biographical information is found.

- Show students the book *The Dot* by Peter H. Reynolds. Share his biographical information. Explain that he is the author as well as the illustrator of the book. Read the book and ask students to recall information about Peter Reynolds.

2. Reading at Home

- Have students choose a book from the library that was written and illustrated by the same person. They take the book home to share with their parents. Together, the parents and child complete the form on page 33. The child returns it to school.

3. Sharing the Book Reports

- Have students sit in a circle holding their completed book report forms. Have a chart ready to record information about the author/illustrators.

- Invite students to share the name of the book they chose and one thing they learned about the author/illustrator.

Good Books to Read

Brown Bear, Brown Bear, What Do You See? and *The Very Hungry Caterpillar* by Eric Carle

A Color of His Own and *Frederick* by Leo Lionni

Count! and *Lunch* by Denise Fleming

The Dot and *ish* by Peter H. Reynolds

Eating the Alphabet and *Planting a Rainbow* by Lois Ehlert

Freight Train and *Flying* by Donald Crews

From Pictures to Words: A Book About Making a Book and *Tops & Bottoms* by Janet Stevens

Name _____

Making Pictures
Book Report Form

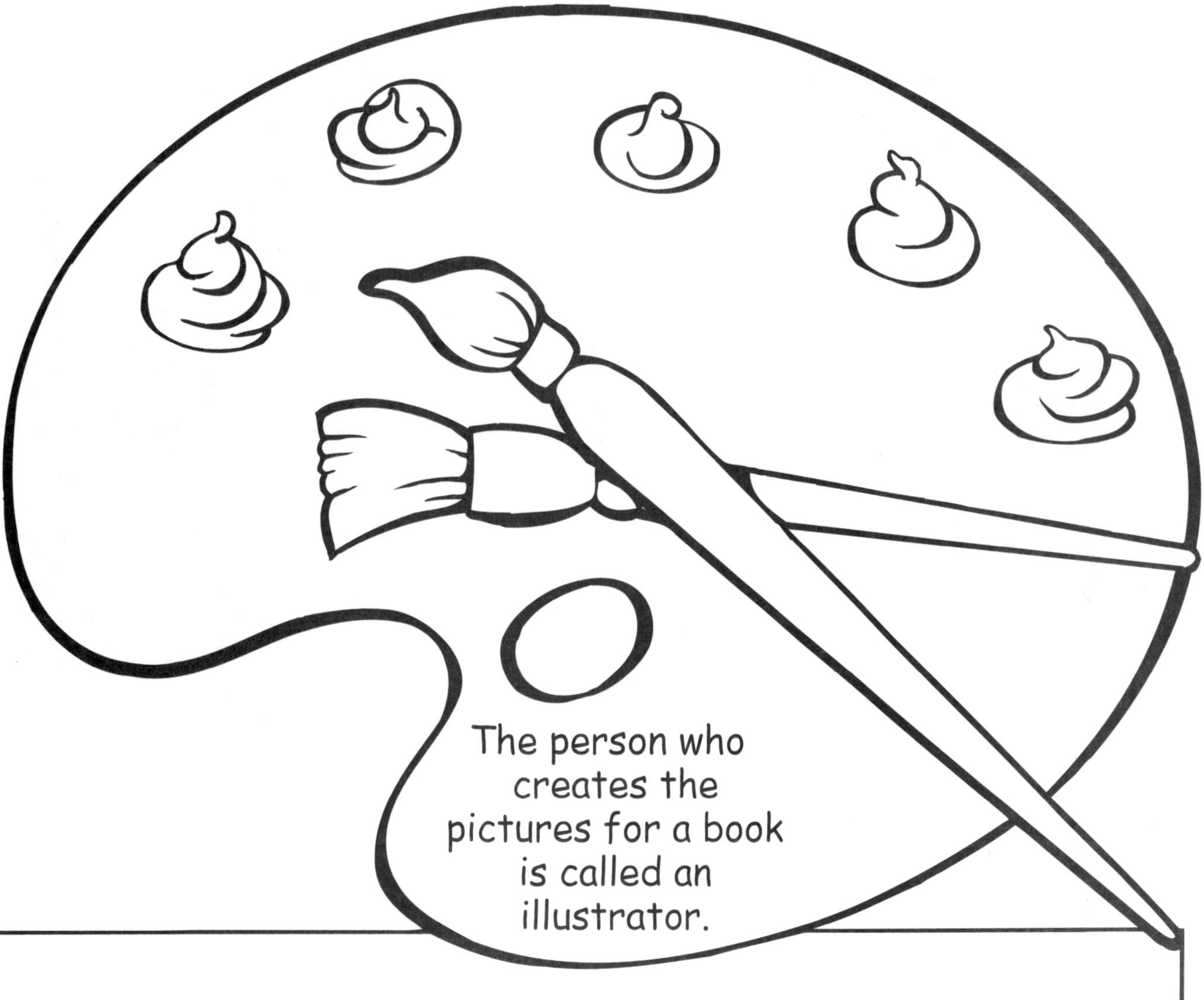

The person who creates the pictures for a book is called an illustrator.

Title: _____

Author/illustrator: _____

I like the pictures in this book.   yes   no

I learned this about the author/illustrator: _____

_____

Dear Parents,
Read this book with your child. Talk about the illustrations in the book. Decide if they are an important part of the story.
Read the information about the author/illustrator. Fill in the report form.

This book report is due back in class: _____   Parent Signature _____

Evaluating a Book

Book Report Form

Literature Skill Focus: Judging a book

1. Reading at School

- Explain to students that they will be judging the books they read this week. They will tell if they like the books. Tell students that this is called an opinion.

- Assure students that there is not one right answer. One student may like a book while another does not.

2. Reading at Home

- Have students choose a book from the library. They take the book home to share with their parents. Together, the parents and child complete the form on page 35. The child returns it to school.

3. Sharing the Book Reports

- Have students sit in a circle holding their completed book report forms.

- Invite students to share the name of the book they chose and a simple evaluation of the book.

Good Books to Read

All About Frogs by Jim Arnosky

Ginger by Charlotte Voake

Grandfather's Journey by Allen Say

Horton Hears a Who! by Dr. Seuss

Jimmy's Boa and the Big Splash Birthday Bash by Trinka Hakes Noble

Joseph Had a Little Overcoat by Simms Taback

Owen by Kevin Henkes

Owl Moon by Jane Yolen

Seven Blind Mice by Ed Young

The Story of Jumping Mouse by John Steptoe

What Do You Do With a Tail Like This? by Robin Page

Where the Wild Things Are by Maurice Sendak

Zinnia and Dot by Lisa Campbell Ernst

Name _____

Evaluating a Book
Book Report Form

Title: _____

Author: _____

Illustrator: _____

____ I like this book.   ____ I don't like this book.

Here is the best part of this book: _____

_____

_____

Dear Parents,
Read this book with your child. Help your child evaluate the book by thinking about whether he or she liked it.
Have your child draw or write about what he or she considers the best part of the book. Fill in the report form.

This book report is due back in class: _____   Parent Signature _____

Recommending a Book
Book Report Form

Literature Skill Focus: Recommending a book to a friend

1. Reading at School

- Explain to students that they will be giving a recommendation on the books they read this week. Discuss with students what comments would be appropriate.

- Tell students that you are asking for their opinion, so there is not one right answer. One student may like a book while another does not.

2. Reading at Home

- Have students choose a book from the library. They take the book home to share with their parents. Together, the parents and child complete the form on page 37. The child returns it to school.

3. Sharing the Book Reports

- Have students sit in a circle holding their completed book reports forms.

- Invite students to share the name of the book they chose and tell whether they would recommend it to a friend. Encourage students to support their opinions by telling why or why not.

Good Books to Read

Caterpillars by Claire Llewellyn

Giggle, Giggle, Quack by Doreen Cronin

Jitterbug Jam by Barbara Jean Hicks

Knick-Knack Paddywhack! by Paul O. Zelinsky

Little Quack by Lauren Thompson

Miss Bindergarten's Wild Day by Joseph Slate

Oh, David! by David Shannon

The Pocket Dogs by Margaret Wild and Stephen Michael King

Tanglebird by Bernard Lodge

Time for Bed by Mem Fox

The Tiny Seed by Eric Carle

Waddle, Waddle, Quack, Quack, Quack by Barbara Anne Skalak

Why Can't I Fly? by Rita Golden Gelman and Jack Kent

Name _____

Recommending a Book
Book Report Form

The title of my book is _____

The author is _____

I **would** **would not**   recommend this book to my friend.

This is why: _____

_____

_____

Dear Parents,
Read this book with your child. Talk about whether he or she would recommend the book to a friend. Encourage your child to tell why he or she feels that way. Fill in the report form.

This book report is due back in class: _____   Parent Signature _____

Parent Letter
Support Reading at Home

Dear Parents,

One of the most important things you can do with your child is read together. Read this book with your child. Then complete the report about the book. Feel free to read the book several times if you and your child are enjoying the story. Ask your child to tell about what happened in the book. Talk about why the two of you liked or disliked the story. Retelling a story and evaluating a book are important prereading skills.

Thank you for your help. You are an important part of your child's learning team.

Sincerely,

Dear Parents,

One of the most important things you can do with your child is read together. Read this book with your child. Then complete the report about the book. Feel free to read the book several times if you and your child are enjoying the story. Ask your child to tell about what happened in the book. Talk about why the two of you liked or disliked the story. Retelling a story and evaluating a book are important prereading skills.

Thank you for your help. You are an important part of your child's learning team.

Sincerely,

How to Report on Books • EMC 6007 • © Evan-Moor Corp.

Book Report Projects

Five Little Monkeys Jumping on the Bed

Book Report Project

Literature Skill Focus: Recalling story details through dramatic play

1. Reading at School

- Read *Five Little Monkeys Jumping on the Bed* by Eileen Christelow. Ask students to think about the things the monkeys in the story did. Call on students to act out one thing (jump on the bed, fall off the bed, go to sleep). Other students name the action.

- Have students make the monkey headbands.

- Have students act out the Five Little Monkeys story while wearing their headbands. Take photographs of the "monkeys" as they perform.

2. Reading at Home

- Have students choose a book about monkeys from the library. They take the book, the monkey headband, and the letter on page 96 home.

- After reading the book with his or her child, the parent signs the note. The child returns the letter and the book to school.

Monkey Headband

1. Reproduce page 41 for each student.

2. Students color the monkey.

3. Students cut along the dotted lines.

4. They glue the label to a 3" x 12" (7.5 x 30.5 cm) strip of construction paper.

5. Staple one side of the paper to the monkey.

6. Adjust the strip so that the headband fits the student, and then staple the other side.

How to Report on Books • EMC 6007 • © Evan-Moor Corp.

Five Little Monkeys Jumping on the Bed
Book Report Project

Staple here

Staple here

Reading about monkeys is fun!

We read *Five Little Monkeys Jumping on the Bed* by Eileen Christelow.

My Name: _____

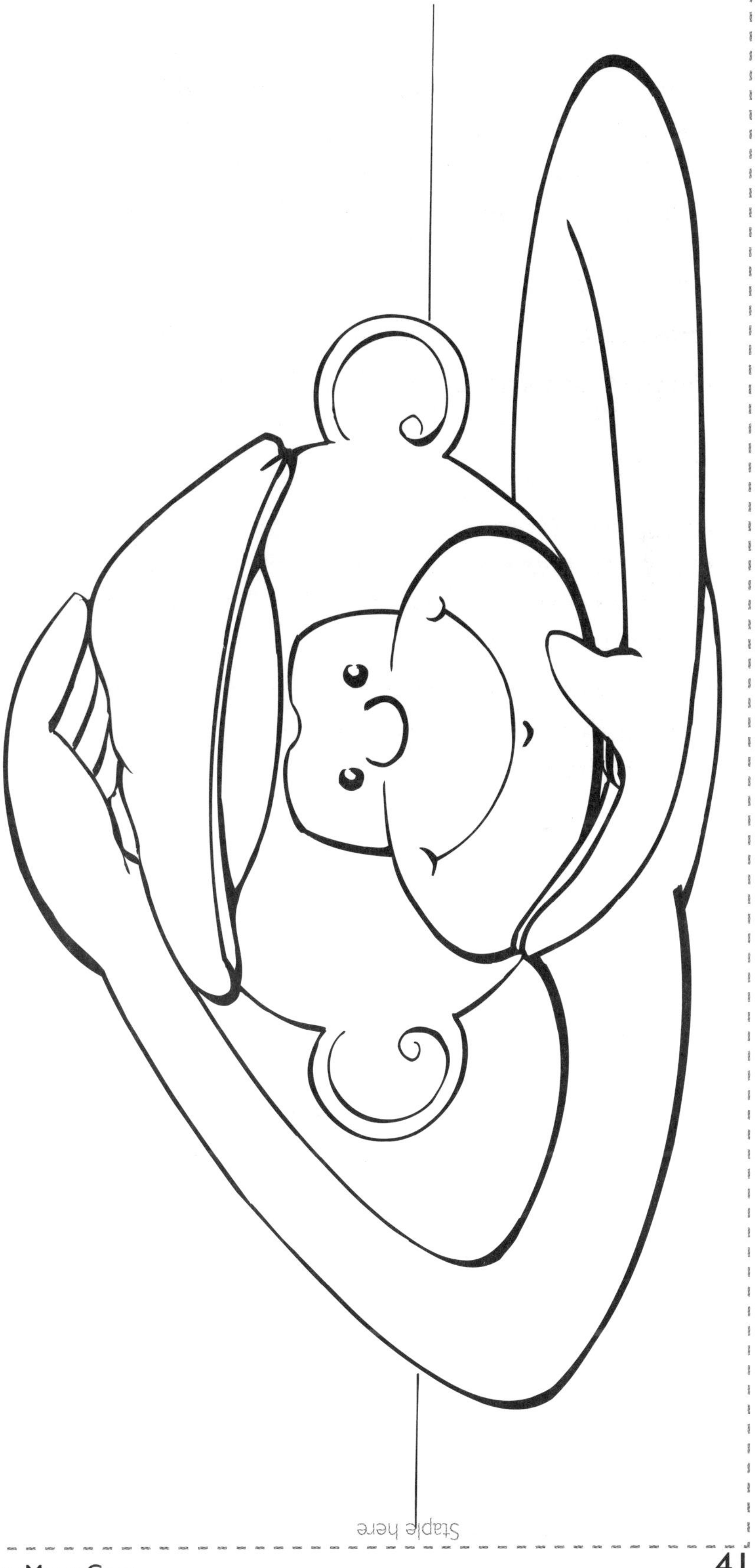

Staple here

Staple here

Where's Spot?

Book Report Project

Literature Skill Focus: Imagining new actions for a character

1. Reading at School

- Read *Where's Spot?* by Eric Hill. Ask students to think about places that Spot might hide. Designate a new location—the classroom, the lunchroom, the playground, or the farm. Have students name new hiding places for Spot.

- Have students make the "Where's Spot?" page.

- Have students sit in a circle with their "Where's Spot?" pages. Invite students to share their imagined hiding places with the group.

2. Reading at Home

- Have students choose a book about dogs from the library. They take the book, their copy of the "Where's Spot?" page, and the note on page 96 home.

- After reading the book with his or her child, the parent signs the note. The child returns the note and the book to school.

Flap Activity

1. Reproduce page 43 for students.

2. Cut one 4" x 5" (10 x 13 cm) rectangle of white construction paper for each student.

3. Students color Spot and his mother.

4. Students glue the white rectangle as indicated on the page.

5. Students draw Spot's hiding place on the white rectangle.

Where's Spot?
Book Report Project

Lift the flap.
What do you see?

We read
Where's Spot?
by Eric Hill.

Glue flap here

My Name _____

The Very Hungry Caterpillar

Book Report Project

Literature Skill Focus: Retelling a story

1. Reading at School

- Read *The Very Hungry Caterpillar* by Eric Carle. Ask students to recall the things the caterpillar ate. On a chart, draw pictures to show the things students remember. Label each picture. Have students retell the story using the chart as a prompt.

- Have students make the caterpillar cutout.

- Have students sit in a circle with their caterpillars. Begin rereading *The Very Hungry Caterpillar*. Pause each time the caterpillar eats something and have students name the snack.

2. Reading at Home

- Have students choose a book about caterpillars from the library. They take the book, the caterpillar cutout, and the note on page 96 home to share.

- After reading the book with his or her child, the parent signs the note. The child returns the note and the book to school.

Caterpillar Cutout

1. Reproduce page 45 for students.

2. Students color the caterpillar and the fruits.

3. Students cut out the shapes along the dotted lines.

4. Cut slits in the fruits using the dotted lines as guides.

5. Students slide the caterpillar through the fruits.

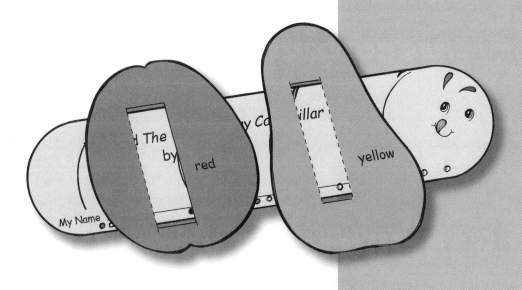

The Very Hungry Caterpillar
Book Report Project

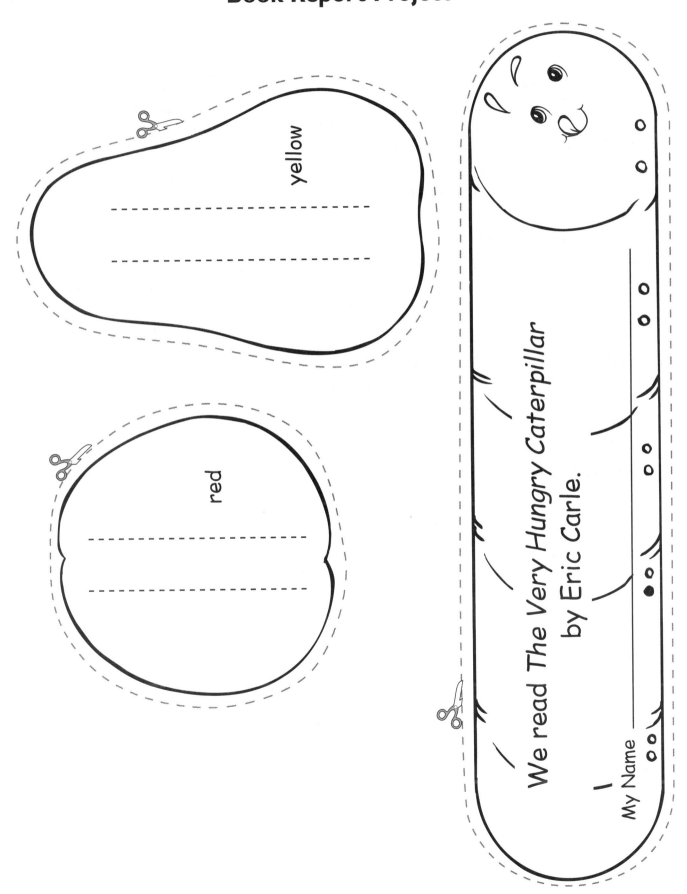

yellow

red

We read The Very Hungry Caterpillar by Eric Carle.

My Name

The Mystery of the Missing Red Mitten
Book Report Project

Literature Skill Focus: Giving clues to a location

1. Reading at School

- Hide a mitten in the classroom. Read *The Mystery of the Missing Red Mitten* by Steven Kellogg.

- Ask students if they have ever lost an item of clothing. Discuss their experiences. Explain that you have hidden a mitten somewhere in the classroom. Have a student look for the mitten. Give clues about the location of the mitten and call out "warm" or "cold" as the student looks.

- Have students make the mitten for the Missing Mitten Game.

2. Reading at Home

- Have students choose a book about mittens from the library. They take the book, the Missing Mitten Game, and the note on page 96 home.

- After reading the book with his or her child, the parent signs the note. The child returns the note and the book to school.

Missing Mitten Game

1. Reproduce page 47 for students.

2. Students color the mitten.

3. Students cut out the mitten along the dotted lines.

4. Students fold the mitten in half and glue it along the open edge, leaving the mitten cuff open.

5. Students play the mitten game, following the directions on the mitten.

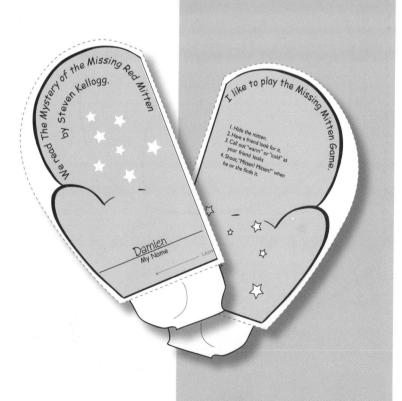

How to Report on Books • EMC 6007 • © Evan-Moor Corp.

The Mystery of the Missing Red Mitten
Book Report Project

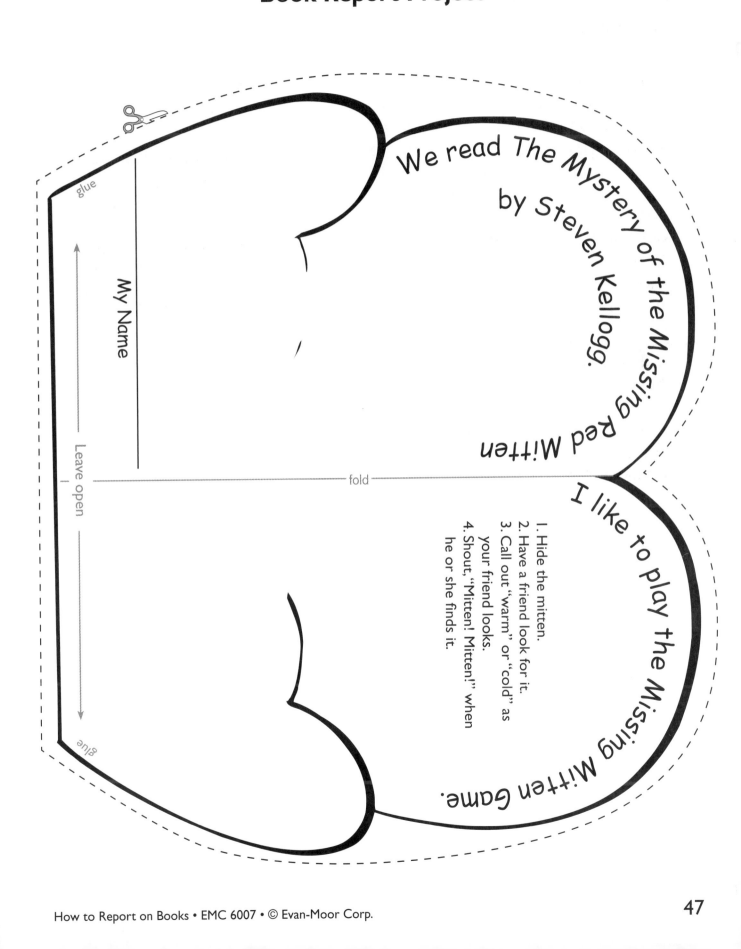

glue

My Name

Leave open

glue

fold

We read *The Mystery of the Missing Red Mitten* by *Steven Kellogg.*

I like to play the *Missing Mitten Game.*

1. Hide the mitten.
2. Have a friend look for it.
3. Call out "warm" or "cold" as your friend looks.
4. Shout, "Mitten! Mitten!" when he or she finds it.

Millions of Cats

Book Report Project

Literature Skill Focus: Describing a character

1. Reading at School

- Read *Millions of Cats* by Wanda Gag. Hold up one of the pages showing several cats. Describe one cat and ask students to identify the cat you have described. Let some students take turns describing one cat on a page while the others listen, look, and identify the cat described.

- Have students make the cat cutout.

- Have students sit in a circle. Make a parade of the cutout cats in the center of the circle. Let students take turns describing a cat while others identify the cat described.

2. Reading at Home

- Students choose a book about cats from the library. They take the book, the cat cutout, and the note on page 96 home.

- After reading the book with his or her child, the parent signs the note. The child returns the note and the book to school.

Cat Cutout

1. Reproduce page 49 for students.

2. Students color and cut out the shapes.

3. Students fold the tail in an accordion fold.

4. Students glue the shapes to an 8½" (21.5 cm) square of colored construction paper.

Millions of Cats
Book Report Project

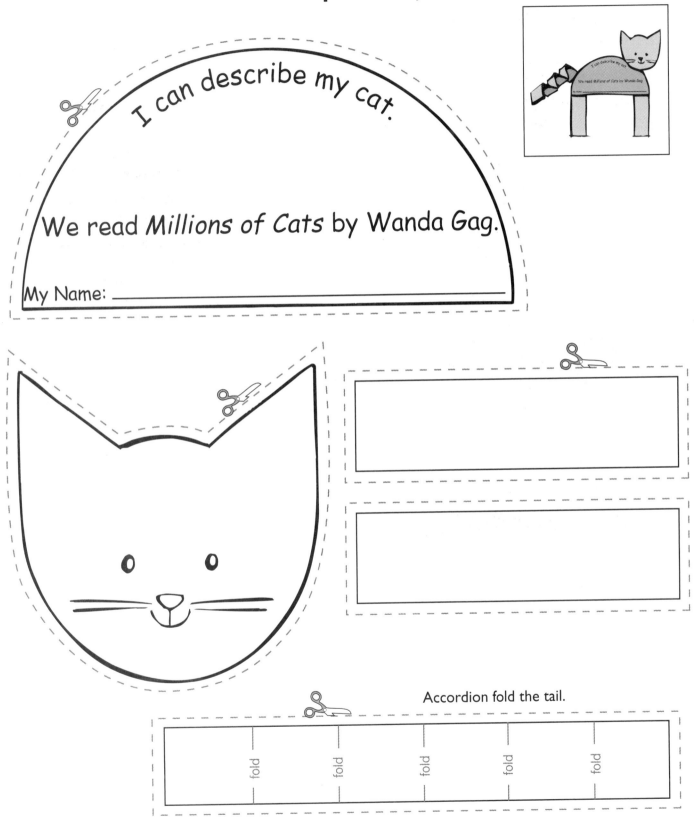

I can describe my cat.

We read *Millions of Cats* by Wanda Gag.

My Name: _____

Accordion fold the tail.

fold   fold   fold   fold   fold

The Napping House

Book Report Project

Literature Skill Focus: Sequencing story events

1. Reading at School

- Read *The Napping House* by Audrey and Don Wood. Ask students to recall the pile of sleepers in the bed. List the sleepers in order on a chart. Have students notice that the largest sleeper is at the bottom and that the sleepers become smaller as they get closer to the top.

- Have students do the cut-and-paste activity to create the pile of napping characters.

2. Reading at Home

- Students choose a book about napping, sleeping, or beds from the library. They take the book, the napping cut-and-paste page, and the note on page 96 home.

- After reading the book with his or her child, the parent signs the note. The child returns the note and the book to school.

Cut-and-Paste Page

1. Reproduce the boxes at the bottom of this page and page 51 for students.

2. Students color the bed and the sleepers.

3. Students cut out the sleepers.

4. They glue them in the appropriate spaces.

5. Students draw a flea on top of the pile.

The Napping House
Book Report Project

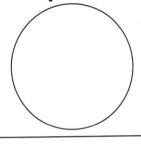

Draw the flea.

We read
The Napping House
by Audrey and
Don Wood.

glue

glue

glue

glue

Who is sleeping in the Napping House?

My Name _____

Katy No-Pocket

Book Report Project

Literature Skill Focus: Identifying the problem and solution in a story

1. Reading at School

- Read *Katy No-Pocket* by Emmy Payne. Ask students to tell what problem Katy faced. Discuss how Katy tried to solve her problem and what the final solution was. Ask students to think about the things they could carry in a pocket.

- Have students make the pocket.

- Have students sit in a circle with their pocket cutouts. Invite students to share with the group the things they drew inside their pockets.

2. Reading at Home

- Have students choose a book about pockets from the library. They take the book, the pocket cutout, and the note on page **96** home to share.

- After reading the book with his or her child, the parent signs the note. The child returns the note and the book to school.

The Pocket

1. Reproduce page 53 for students.

2. Students color and cut out the pocket.

3. Students fold the pocket.

4. On the inside flap, students draw and color something they would like to put in their pocket.

Ricardo
My Name

We read *Katy No-Pocket* by Emmy Payne.

Guess what I have in this pocket.

How to Report on Books • EMC 6007 • © Evan-Moor Corp.

Katy No-Pocket
Book Report Project

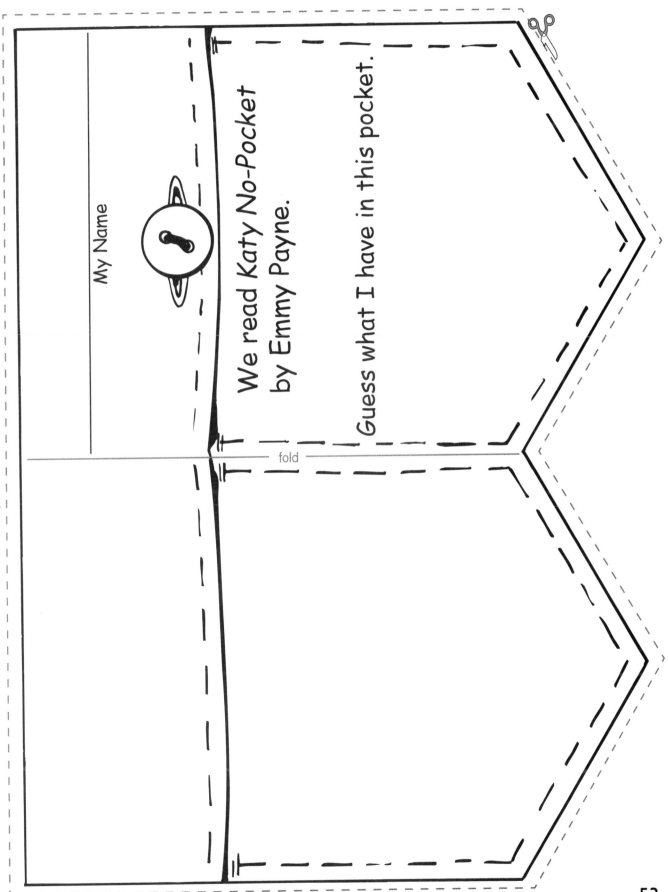

My Name

We read Katy No-Pocket by Emmy Payne.

Guess what I have in this pocket.

fold

Harry the Dirty Dog

Book Report Project

Literature Skill Focus: Retelling a story with a puppet

1. Reading at School

- Make a dog puppet with a clean dog on one side and a dirty dog on the other side. Read *Harry the Dirty Dog* by Gene Zion. Have one student put the puppet on his or her hand. Retell the story. Have the student turn the puppet back and forth as Harry changes from clean to dirty to clean.

- Have students make the dog puppet.

2. Reading at Home

- Have students choose a book about dogs from the library. They take the book, the dog puppet, and the note on page 96 home to share.

- After reading the book with his or her child, the parent signs the note. The child returns the note and the book to school.

Dog Puppet

1. Reproduce page 55 for students.

2. Students color and cut out the puppet.

3. Students fold the puppet in half.

4. They glue it along the open edge, leaving the bottom open.

5. Students glue the ears to the puppet.

Harry the Dirty Dog
Book Report Project

We read *Harry the Dirty Dog* by Gene Zion.

glue

glue

dirty

fold

My Name _____

clean

glue

Where's the Big Bad Wolf?

Book Report Project

Literature Skill Focus: Describing a character and predicting its actions

1. Reading at School

- Read *Where's the Big Bad Wolf?* by Eileen Christelow. Ask students to describe the wolf. Record their words and phrases on a chart.

- Ask students to predict if the Big Bad Wolf would do the following things: host a tea party, play tricks on a hen, wear a costume to get inside the little pig's house, take ballet classes, practice good table manners, or go to school.

- Have students make the Big Bad Wolf puppet.

2. Reading at Home

- Have students choose a book about a big bad wolf from the library. They take the book, the puppet, and the note on page 96 home to share.

- After reading the book with his or her child, the parent signs the note. The child returns the note and the book to school.

Wolf Puppet

1. Reproduce page 57 for students.

2. Students color the wolf.

3. Students cut out the puppet along the dotted lines.

4. Students fold the puppet in half and glue it along the open edge, leaving the bottom open.

How to Report on Books • EMC 6007 • © Evan-Moor Corp.

Where's the Big Bad Wolf?
Book Report Project

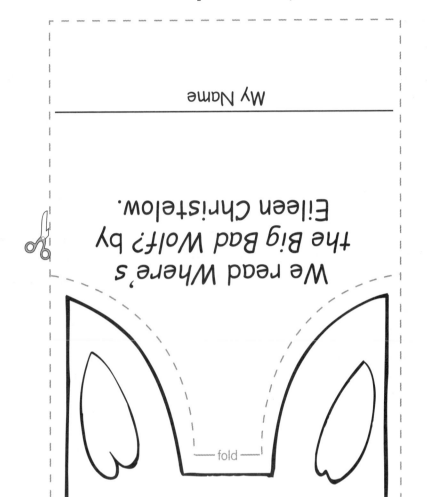

My Name

We read Where's the Big Bad Wolf? by Eileen Christelow.

fold

glue

glue

A Red Wagon Year

Book Report Project

Literature Skill Focus: Identifying the setting of a story

1. Reading at School

- Read *A Red Wagon Year* by Kathi Appelt. Ask students to tell where the story took place. Then ask students to tell when the story took place. Introduce the term *setting* if it is appropriate for your students.

- Ask students if the story took place in just one time or if the time changed during the story. Explain that some stories take place over a short time and some over a long time. Discuss the different ways that the wagon was used each month.

- Have students make the wagon spinner. Ask them to draw a passenger in the wagon. Tell students to decorate the wagon as it was decorated during their favorite month in the story.

2. Reading at Home

- Have students choose a book about wagons from the library. They take the book, the wagon spinner, and the note on page 96 home to share.

- After reading the book with his or her child, the parent signs the note. The child returns the note and the book to school.

Wagon Spinner

1. Reproduce page 59 for students.

2. Provide a 9" (23 cm) paper plate and a paper fastener for each student.

3. Students color the wagon and draw a passenger in it. They fill in the book information.

4. Students cut out the forms.

5. Using the paper fastener, fasten the wagon to the paper plate. Glue the label to the plate.

6. Students write their names on the paper plate.

A Red Wagon Year
Book Report Project

We read *A Red Wagon Year* by Kathi Appelt.

I'm riding my way through good books!

Title:

Author:

Illustrator:

Little Grunt and the Big Egg

Book Report Project

Literature Skill Focus: Identifying the problem and solution in a story

1. Reading at School

• Read *Little Grunt and the Big Egg: A Prehistoric Fairy Tale* by Tomie dePaola. Ask students what problems Little Grunt faced. (First, Little Grunt had to find some eggs. Then Little Grunt's pet dinosaur grew too big.) Have students explain how the problems in the story were solved.

• Have students make the cave. Ask students to draw George and Little Grunt inside the cave.

2. Reading at Home

• Have students choose a book about caves from the library. They take the book, the cave flap page, and the note on page 96 home to share.

• After reading the book with his or her child, the parent signs the note. The child returns the note and the book to school.

The Cave

1. Reproduce page 61 for students.

2. Provide a 9" x 12" (23 x 30.5 cm) sheet of yellow construction paper for each student.

3. Students color the cave.

4. Students cut out and fold open the cave door.

5. Students glue the cave to the yellow construction paper.

6. Students draw George and Little Grunt inside the cave.

Little Grunt and the Big Egg
Book Report Project

My Name _____

We read Little Grunt and the Big Egg.

Can you guess who is in this cave?

fold

Buzz Buzz Buzz

Book Report Project

Literature Skill Focus: Using sound words (onomatopoeia) to retell a story

1. Reading at School

- Read *Buzz Buzz Buzz* by Byron Barton. Ask students to name the characters in the story. List the characters on a chart. As you point to each character, have students make the sound associated with that character.

- Assign one student to each character. Retell the story, and when you say a character's name, have the student representing that character make the character's sound.

- Have students make the barn cutout.

2. Reading at Home

- Have students choose a book about barns from the library. They take the book, the barn cutout, and the note on page 96 home to share.

- After reading the book with his or her child, the parent signs the note. The child returns the note and the book to school.

The Barn

1. Reproduce page 63 for students.

2. Students color and cut out the barn and the picture strip.

3. Cut the slits in the barn doorway.

4. Students slip the strip through the slits to show who is in the barn.

How to Report on Books • EMC 6007 • © Evan-Moor Corp.

Buzz Buzz Buzz
Book Report Project

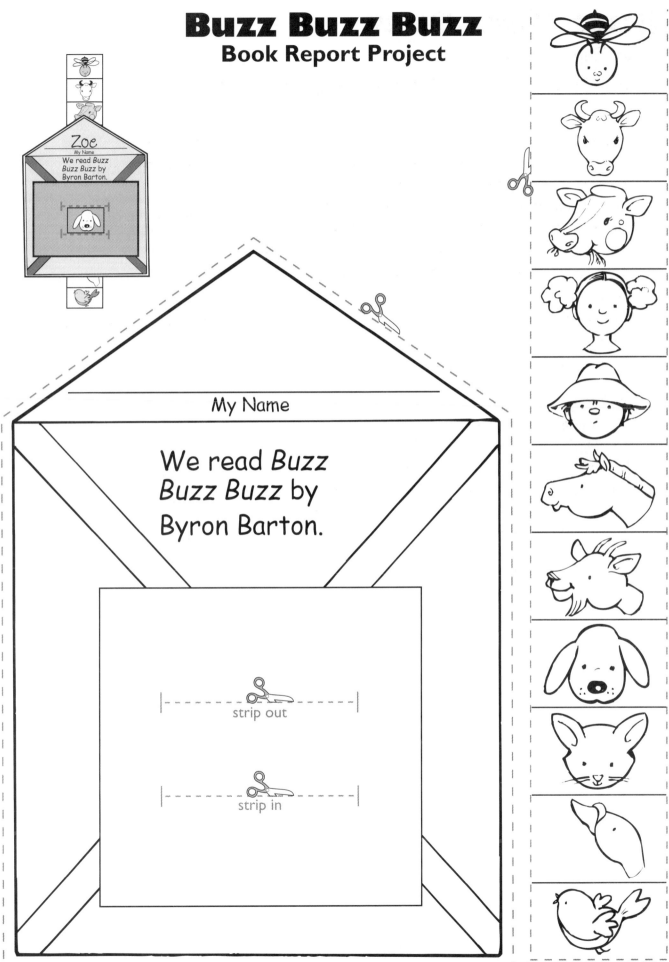

My Name

We read *Buzz Buzz Buzz* by Byron Barton.

strip out

strip in

Little Rabbit's Loose Tooth

Book Report Project

Literature Skill Focus: Sequencing story events

1. Reading at School

- Choose a book about losing teeth, such as *Little Rabbit's Loose Tooth* by Lucy Bate. Make several large teeth with illustrations showing important events in the story. Put the teeth in a large envelope.

- Read the book to the students. Display the tooth pictures. Ask students to pick the picture that represents the thing that happened first. Continue identifying pictures and putting them in chronological order.

- Have students make the lost tooth envelope.

2. Reading at Home

- Have students choose a book about losing teeth from the library. They take the book, the lost tooth envelope, and the note on page 96 home to share.

- After reading the book with his or her child, the parent signs the note. The child returns the note and the book to school.

Lost Tooth Envelope

1. Reproduce page 65 for students.

2. Students color the tooth envelope.

3. Students cut out the envelope along the dotted lines.

4. Students fold the envelope and glue the sides as shown.

How to Report on Books • EMC 6007 • © Evan-Moor Corp.

Little Rabbit's Loose Tooth
Book Report Project

I read a book about losing a tooth.

fold

We read
Little Rabbit's Loose Tooth by
Lucy Bate.

glue

glue

My Name _____

fold

glue

fold

fold

glue

Ira Sleeps Over
Book Report Project

Literature Skill Focus: Relating story events to personal experiences

1. Reading at School

- Read *Ira Sleeps Over* by Bernard Waber. Ask students if they have ever slept over at someone else's house. Discuss their experiences. Ask them if they took something special with them.

- Have students draw a picture of something that is special to them. Label each drawing with a sentence that tells about the special thing. Bind the pictures into a class book entitled *Our Special Things*.

- Have students make the bear puzzle.

2. Reading at Home

- Have students choose a book about a special thing from the library. They take the book, the bear puzzle, and the note on page 96 home to share.

- After reading the book with his or her child, the parent signs the note. The child returns the note and the book to school.

Bear Puzzle

1. Reproduce page 67 for students.

2. Provide each student with an 8½" (21.5 cm) square of construction paper.

3. Students color and cut out the puzzle pieces.

4. Each student glues the puzzle together on the construction paper.

5. Students write their names on the back.

How to Report on Books • EMC 6007 • © Evan-Moor Corp.

Ira Sleeps Over
Book Report Project

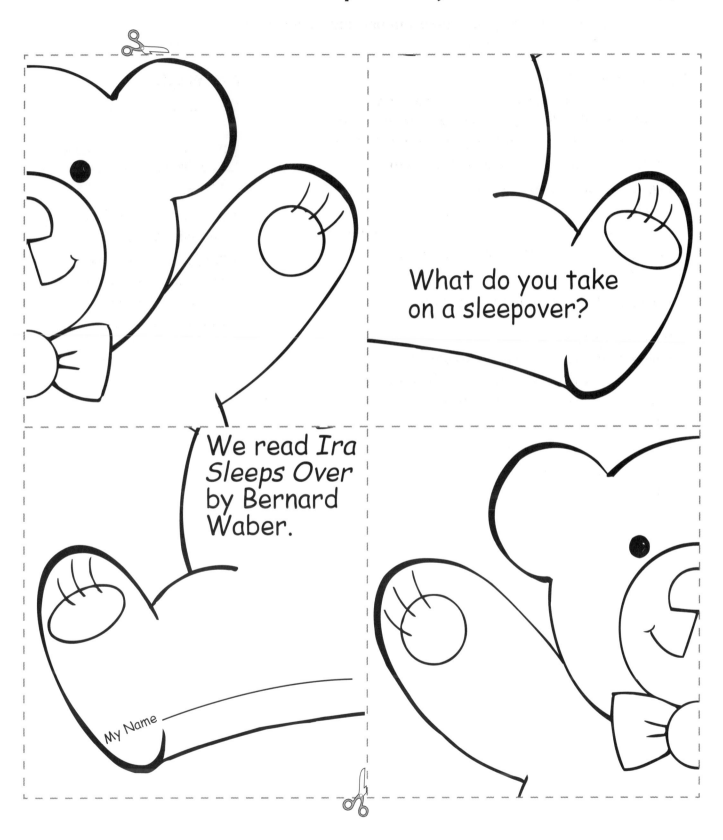

There's a Nightmare in My Closet

Book Report Project

Literature Skill Focus: Determining if a book is real or make-believe

1. Reading at Home

- Review the meaning of the terms *real* and *make-believe*. Read *There's a Nightmare in My Closet* by Mercer Mayer. Ask students if the book tells a real story or a make-believe story.

- Have students identify what makes the story make-believe. Ask students to tell a real story about their bedtime.

- Have students make the closet.

2. Reading at School

- Have students choose a book about closets from the library. They take the book, the closet flap page, and the note on page 96 home to share.

- After reading the book with his or her child, the parent signs the note. The child returns the note and the book to school.

The Closet

1. Reproduce the bottom of this page and page 69 for students.

2. Students color the sleeper, the door, and the closet.

3. Students cut out the closet door along the dotted lines.

4. Students glue the door onto the side of the closet.

5. Ask students to draw something in the closet.

What is in the closet?

How to Report on Books • EMC 6007 • © Evan-Moor Corp.

There's a Nightmare in My Closet
Book Report Project

glue door here

We read *There's a Nightmare in My Closet* by Mercer Mayer.

My Name

Peter's Chair
Book Report Project

Literature Skill Focus: Understanding character motivation

1. Reading at School

• Read *Peter's Chair* by Ezra Jack Keats. Ask students to retell the story. Then ask them why they think Peter took his blue chair and ran away. (He was jealous. He didn't want all of his furniture painted pink.)

• Ask students if they have ever felt jealous of someone. Explain that sometimes authors give their characters real feelings and have them act like real people.

• Have students color the chair on page 71.

2. Reading at Home

• Have students choose a book about chairs from the library. They take the book, the chair page, and the note on page 96 home to share.

• After reading the book with his or her child, the parent signs the note. The child returns the note and the book to school.

The Chair

1. Reproduce page 71 for students.

2. Students color and decorate the chair.

Peter's Chair
Book Report Project

What color would you paint your chair?

We read a book called

Peter's Chair

by Ezra Jack Keats.

My Name _____

Are You My Mother?

Book Report Project

Literature Skill Focus: Predicting what will happen next

1. Reading at School

- Introduce your students to the book *Are You My Mother?* by P. D. Eastman. Explain that you will read a bit and stop so that students can predict what will happen next. Read the book, stopping several times to ask for student predictions.

- Have students make the nest cutout.

2. Reading at Home

- Have students choose a book about nests from the library. They take the book, the nest, and the note on page 96 home to share.

- After reading the book with his or her child, the parent signs the note. The child returns the note and the book to school.

The Nest

1. Reproduce page 73 for students.

2. Students color the bird and the nest.

3. Students color and cut out the pictures.

4. Students glue the pictures to the boxes in the order in which the events in the story happened.

How to Report on Books • EMC 6007 • © Evan-Moor Corp.

Are You My Mother?
Book Report Project

We read
Are You My Mother?
by P. D. Eastman.

Glue the pictures in order.

glue	glue	glue	glue

My Name _____

Tops & Bottoms
Book Report Project

Literature Skill Focus: Comparing characters in a story

1. Reading at School

- Read *Tops & Bottoms* by Janet Stevens. Ask students to think about the two main characters in the story as you read.

- Have students describe the two characters. Record their responses on a chart. Ask students which character they liked better and why.

- Have students make a turnip fold-up.

2. Reading at Home

- Have students choose a book about growing things in a garden from the library. They take the book, the turnip fold-up, and the note on page 96 home to share.

- After reading the book with his or her child, the parent signs the note. The child returns the note and the book to school.

The Turnip

1. Reproduce page 75 for students.

2. Students fold the form on the fold line. Fold it up to hide the turnip. Fold it down to see the turnip.

3. Students color the turnip and the ground. The ground should also be colored on the fold-up flap.

4. Students cut out the turnip along the dotted lines.

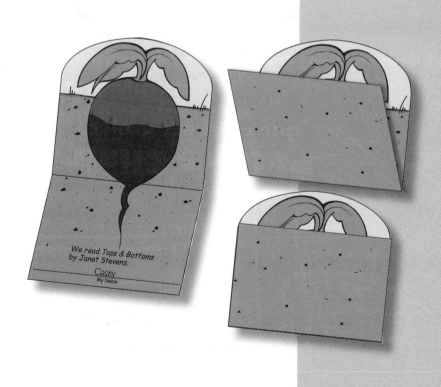

How to Report on Books • EMC 6007 • © Evan-Moor Corp.

Tops & Bottoms
Book Report Project

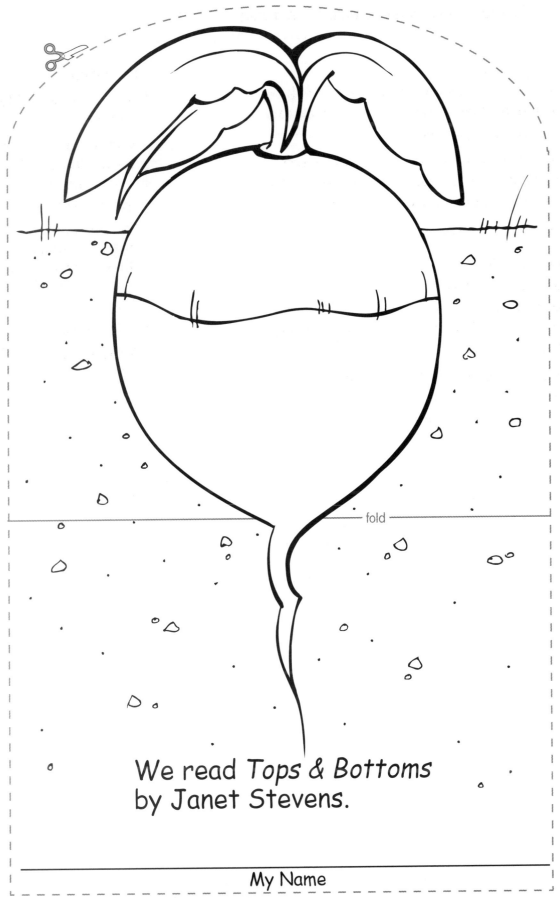

We read *Tops & Bottoms* by Janet Stevens.

fold

My Name

Goodnight Moon
Book Report Project

Literature Skill Focus: Determining if a story is real or make-believe

1. Reading at School

• Read *Goodnight Moon* by Margaret Wise Brown. Ask students if the story is real or make-believe. Have students identify what makes the story imaginary.

• Ask students to tell some of the things that are in their rooms that they could say goodnight to before going to sleep.

• Have students make a moon mobile.

2. Reading at Home

• Have students choose a book about the moon from the library. They take the book, the moon mobile, and the note on page 96 home to share.

• After reading the book with his or her child, the parent signs the note. The child returns the note and the book to school.

Moon Mobile

1. Reproduce page 77 for students.

2. Students color and cut out the moon and the five circles.

3. They glue the moon to a 7" (18 cm) square of black construction paper.

4. Tape a 6" (15 cm) piece of yarn to each circle.

5. Tape each hanging circle to the bottom edge of the paper.

6. Hang the mobile with another piece of yarn that has been taped to the top of the mobile.

Goodnight Moon
Book Report Project

We read Goodnight Moon by Margaret Wise Brown.

My Name

Freight Train
Book Report Project

Literature Skill Focus: Identifying and reading color words

1. Reading at School

- Read *Freight Train* by Donald Crews. Ask students to name the colors of the cars in the freight train. Record the color words on a chart.

- Play a simple game that requires students to read the color words. For example, point to the word *blue* and say, "If your shirt is this color, stand up."

- Have students make the train cutout.

2. Reading at Home

- Students choose a book about trains from the library. They take the book, the train cutout, and the note on page 96 home to share.

- After reading the book with his or her child, the parent signs the note. The child returns the note and the book to school.

Train Cutout

1. Reproduce page 79 for students.

2. Students color and cut out the train cars and the label.

3. Students fold back the bottom edge of the cars.

4. They glue the cars to a 12" x 18" (30.5 x 45.5 cm) sheet of brown construction paper.

5. Then they glue the label to the construction paper.

Freight Train
Book Report Project

Get on the train to good reading!

Fold back and glue.

black

Fold back and glue.

orange

purple

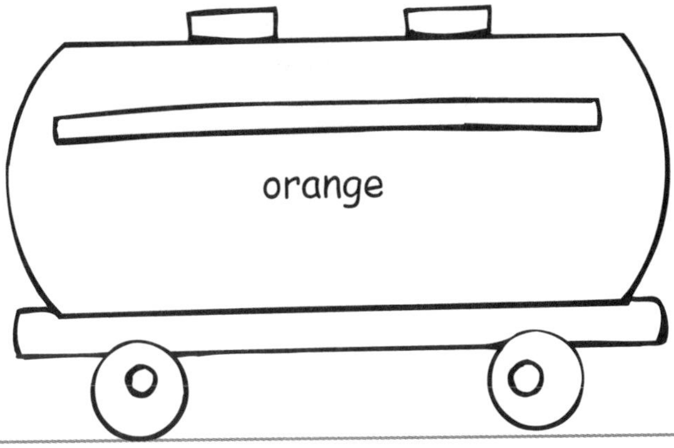

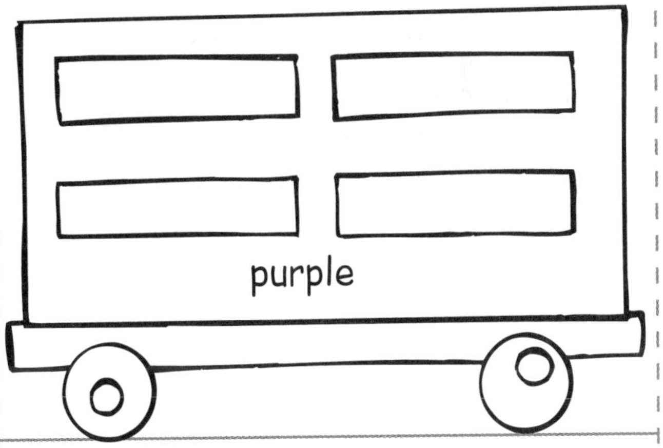

Fold back and glue.

Fold back and glue.

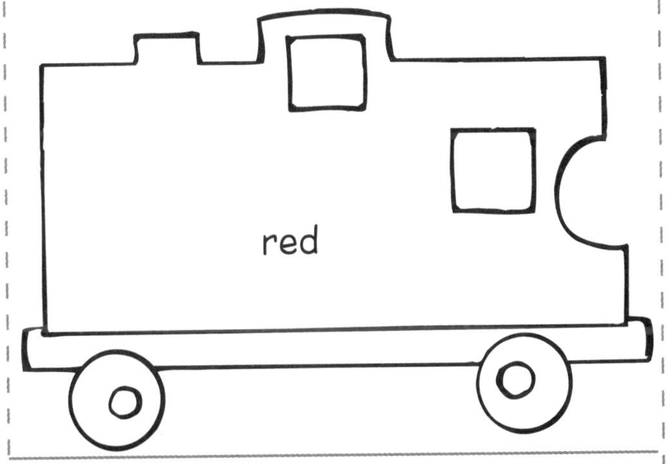

red

We read *Freight Train* by Donald Crews.

Fold back and glue.

_____
My Name

This Little Chick
Book Report Project

Literature Skill Focus: Predicting what will happen next

1. Reading at School

- Show students the book *This Little Chick* by John Lawrence. Tell them the name of the author. Explain that you will read a bit and then stop. Ask students to predict what Little Chick will say next.

- Reread the book with several students acting out the parts of the farm animals.

- Have students make the hatching egg.

2. Reading at Home

- Students choose a book about hatching eggs from the library. They take the book, the hatching egg, and the note on page 96 home to share.

- After reading the book with his or her child, the parent signs the note. The child returns the note and the book to school.

Hatching Egg

1. Reproduce page 81 for students.

2. Students color and cut out the egg pieces.

3. Students glue the cracked shell to the egg as shown.

4. Students fold back the shell to see the chick inside.

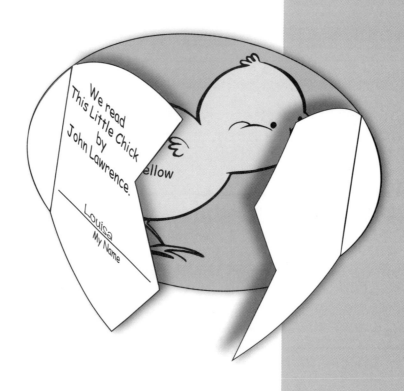

This Little Chick
Book Report Project

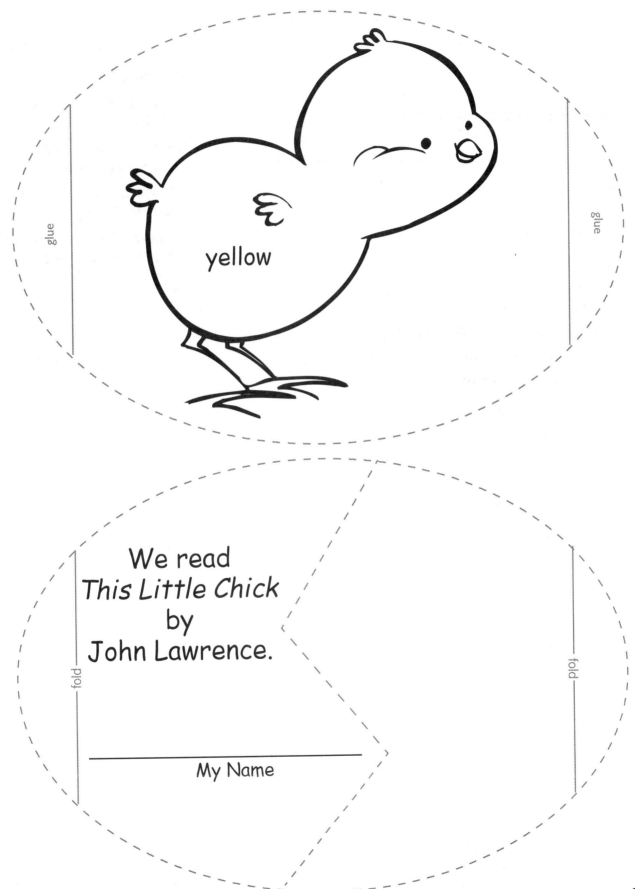

glue

glue

yellow

fold

fold

We read
This Little Chick
by
John Lawrence.

_____
My Name

Happy Birthday, Jesse Bear!
Book Report Project

Literature Skill Focus: Describing a story's setting

1. Reading at School

- Review with students what a setting is—the place and time a story takes place. Read *Happy Birthday, Jesse Bear!* by Nancy White Carlstrom.

- Ask students to describe the place and the time the story takes place. List students' ideas on a chart. Reread the story to see if students can find additional details.

- Have students make the birthday headband.

2. Reading at Home

- Have students choose a book about a birthday celebration from the library. They take the book, the birthday headband, and the note on page 96 home to share.

- After reading the book with his or her child, the parent signs the note. The child returns the note and the book to school.

The Headband

1. Reproduce page 83 for students.

2. Students color and cut out the headband pieces.

3. Students glue the candles to the cake.

4. They glue the happy birthday message to a 3" x 12" (7.5 x 30.5 cm) strip of construction paper.

5. Staple or tape the construction paper strip to one side of the cake.

6. Adjust the headband to fit the child, and then fasten the other side.

We read Happy Birthday, Jesse Bear! by Nancy White Carlstrom.

Happy Birthday, Jesse Bear!
Book Report Project

We read Happy Birthday, Jesse Bear! by Nancy White Carlstrom.

Your birthday headband will look like this!

My Name _____

Happy birthday, everyone!

Kitten's First Full Moon

Book Report Project

Literature Skill Focus: Identifying the main character's problem

1. Reading at School

- Explain to students that usually the main character in a story faces a problem. Ask students to listen for Kitten's problem as you read the book *Kitten's First Full Moon* by Kevin Henkes.

- Ask students what problem Kitten faced. Decide whether Kitten solved her problem during the story.

- Have students make the cat puzzle.

2. Reading at Home

- Students choose a book about cats from the library. They take the book, the cat puzzle, and the note on page 96 home to share.

- After reading the book with his or her child, the parent signs the note. The child returns the note and the book to school.

Cat Puzzle

1. Reproduce page 85 for students.

2. Students color and cut out the three cat pieces.

3. Arrange the pieces to make a cat.

4. Glue the cat pieces to an 8½" x 12" (21.5 x 30.5 cm) sheet of construction paper.

5. Students write their names on the paper.

Kitten's First Full Moon
Book Report Project

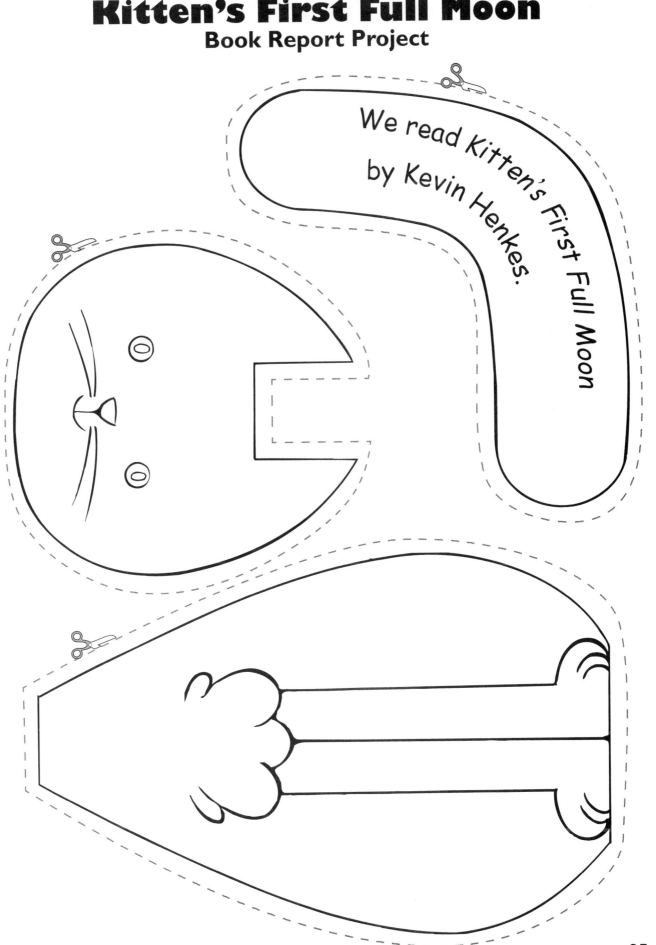

We read Kitten's First Full Moon by Kevin Henkes.

A Boy, a Dog and a Frog
Book Report Project

Literature Skill Focus: Adding words to pictures to tell a story

1. Reading at School

- Show students the first few pages of *A Boy, a Dog and a Frog* by Mercer Mayer. Ask them what they notice about the book. One observation should be that there are no words on the pages. Explain that some authors choose to tell their stories with pictures rather than words.

- Show students each page of the book. Ask them to add words to a few pages to tell the story.

- Have students make the frog headband.

2. Reading at Home

- Students choose a book about frogs from the library. They take the book, the frog headband, and the note on page 96 home to share.

- After reading the book with his or her child, the parent signs the note. The child returns the note and the book to school.

Frog Headband

1. Reproduce page 87 for students.

2. Students color and cut out the frog headband and the label.

3. Students glue the "good reading" label to a 3" x 12" (7.5 x 30.5 cm) strip of green construction paper.

4. Tape or staple one side of the construction paper strip to the frog.

5. Adjust the headband to fit the child, and then fasten the other side.

We read A Boy, a Dog and a Frog by Mercer Mayer.

A Boy, a Dog and a Frog
Book Report Project

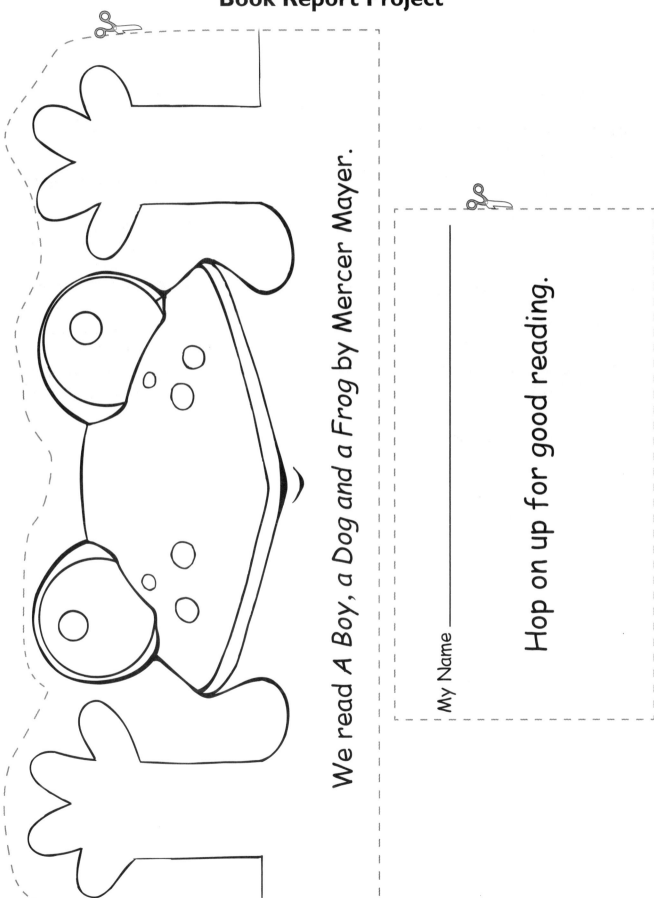

We read *A Boy, a Dog and a Frog* by Mercer Mayer.

My Name

Hop on up for good reading.

Frederick
Book Report Project

Literature Skill Focus: Learning about collage

1. Reading at School

- Show students several pictures from *Frederick* by Leo Lionni. Explain that Leo Lionni made Frederick by tearing and cutting paper. When a picture is made from cut paper and bits of other things, it is called a collage.

- Ask students to look carefully at the illustrations as you read Leo Lionni's book.

- Have students make the mouse picture.

2. Reading at Home

- Students choose a book about a mouse from the library. They take the book, the mouse picture, and the note on page 96 home to share.

- After reading the book with his or her child, the parent signs the note. The child returns the note and the book to school.

A Mouse

1. Reproduce page 89 for students.

2. Students color and cut out the pieces.

3. Students glue the pieces to a 9" (23 cm) square of construction paper.

4. Students add a yarn tail to their mouse picture.

5. Students write their names on the picture.

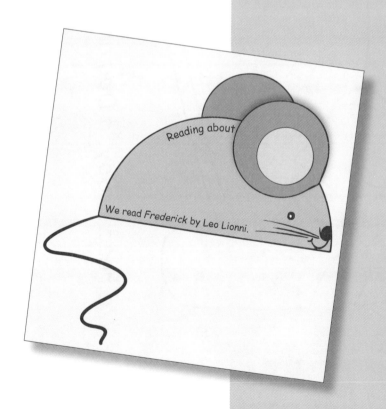

Frederick
Book Report Project

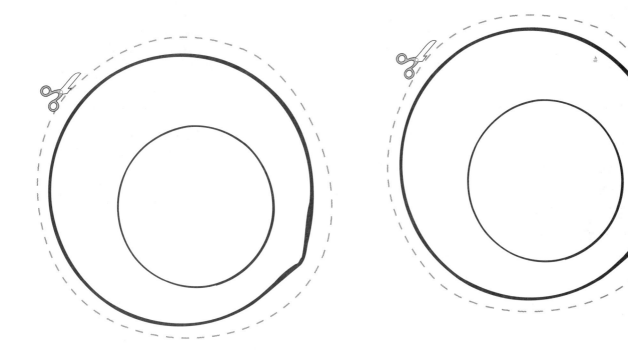

Reading about mice is fun!

We read *Frederick* by Leo Lionni.

The Giant Jam Sandwich

Book Report Project

Literature Skill Focus: Sequencing story details

1. Reading at School

- Read *The Giant Jam Sandwich* by John Vernon Lord. Ask students to recall the ingredients in the giant sandwich. List them on a chart. Number the ingredients to show the order.

- Have students make the slice of bread cutout.

2. Reading at Home

- Students choose a book about food from the library. They take the book, the slice of bread, and the note on page 96 home to share.

- After reading the book with his or her child, the parent signs the note. The child returns the note and the book to school.

Slice of Bread

1. Reproduce page 91 for students.

2. Students color the slice of bread.

3. They color and cut out the pictures of the two ingredients in the sandwich.

4. Students glue the two ingredients to the slice of bread.

How to Report on Books • EMC 6007 • © Evan-Moor Corp.

The Giant Jam Sandwich
Book Report Project

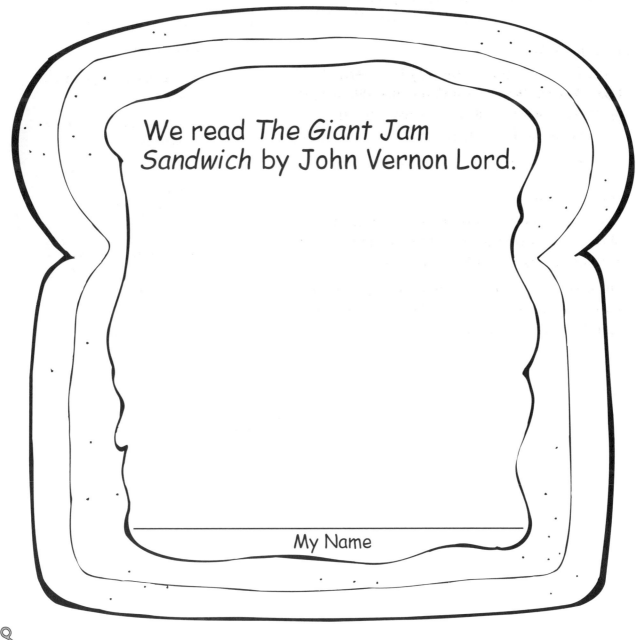

We read *The Giant Jam Sandwich* by John Vernon Lord.

My Name

Where the Wild Things Are

Book Report Project

Literature Skill Focus: Determining if a story is real or make-believe

1. Reading at School

- Review the meaning of the terms *real* and *make-believe*. Explain to students that one way to describe characters in a book would be to tell whether they are real or make-believe.

- Read *Where the Wild Things Are* by Maurice Sendak. Ask students to tell you the characters in the book. List the students' responses. Then decide whether each character is real or make-believe.

- Have students make the monster mask.

2. Reading at Home

- Students choose a book about monsters from the library. They take the book, the monster mask, and the note on page 96 home to share.

- After reading the book with his or her child, the parent signs the note. The child returns the note and the book to school.

Monster Mask

1. Reproduce page 93 for students.

2. Students color and cut out the mask.

3. Students glue the mask to a 7½" x 8½" (19 x 21.5 cm) sheet of construction paper.

4. Students write their names on the back of the paper.

5. Cut out eye holes for each student.

6. Punch holes as shown and attach yarn to each side.

Where the Wild Things Are
Book Report Project

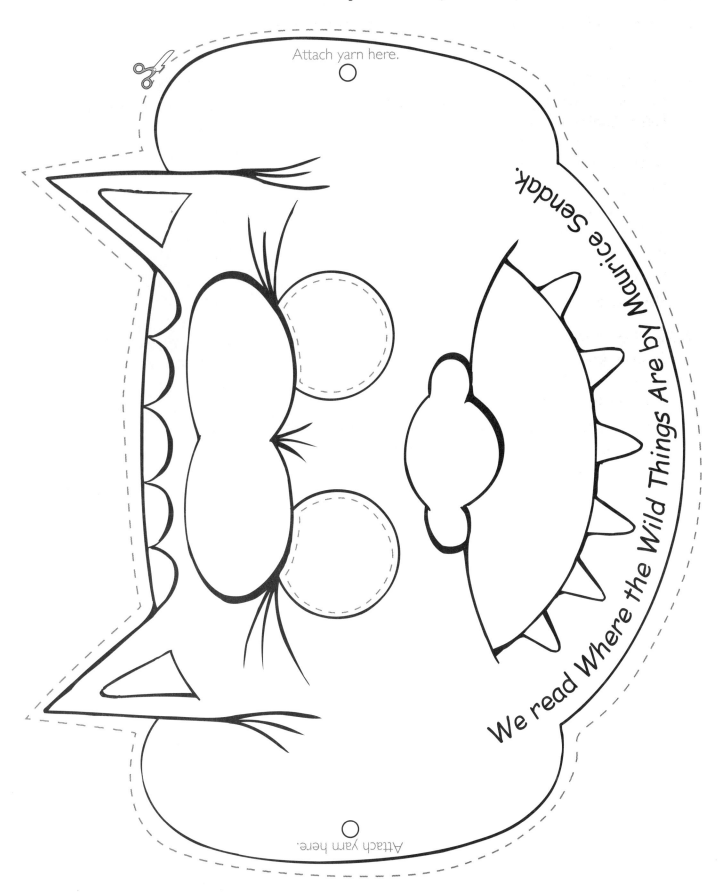

Attach yarn here.

We read Where the Wild Things Are by Maurice Sendak.

Attach yarn here.

The Gingerbread Boy

Book Report Project

Literature Skill Focus: Recalling story details through dramatic play

1. Reading at School

- Read *The Gingerbread Boy* by Paul Galdone or Richard Egielski.

- Assign parts and have students act out the story. At first, provide the narration to tell what the characters are doing. Have the characters repeat the refrains. Then let the characters act out the complete story.

- Have students make the gingerbread boy puppets.

2. Reading at Home

- Students choose a book about a gingerbread character from the library. They take the book, the puppet, and the note on page 96 home to share.

- After reading the book with his or her child, the parent signs the note. The child returns the note and the book to school.

Gingerbread Boy Puppet

1. Reproduce page 95 on white construction paper for students.

2. Provide two paper fasteners and a straw for each student.

3. Students color and cut out the puppet.

4. Students attach the puppet's arms with paper fasteners.

5. Students tape a straw to the back of the puppet.

Run, run, as fast as you can. You can't catch me. I'm the Gingerbread Man!

Mollie

My Name

How to Report on Books • EMC 6007 • © Evan-Moor Corp.

The Gingerbread Boy
Book Report Project

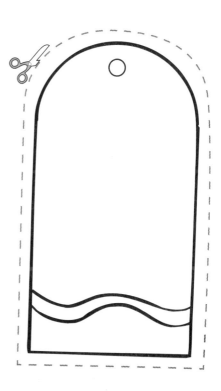

Run, run, as fast as you can. You can't catch me.

I'm the Gingerbread Man!

My Name

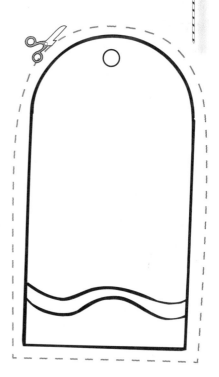

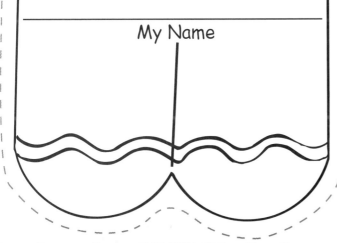

Parent Letter
Support Reading at Home

Dear Parents,

We created this project today in response to a book we read together in class. Ask your child to tell you all about it. Your child chose another book to read at home. Please read this book with your child. Fill out the bottom of this note and return it with the book.

Thank you for encouraging your child's love of reading.

Sincerely,

We read _____

by _____.

We   liked   disliked   the book.

Student's Name _____

Dear Parents,

We created this project today in response to a book we read together in class. Ask your child to tell you all about it. Your child chose another book to read at home. Please read this book with your child. Fill out the bottom of this note and return it with the book.

Thank you for encouraging your child's love of reading.

Sincerely,

We read _____

by _____.

We   liked   disliked   the book.

Student's Name _____